Tres cuentos para aprender inglés

Edición bilingüe

con los textos en inglés y español

By

Noreen J. Byrne

Noreen J. Byrne. Diplomada en Inglés y Literatura y Certificado T.E.F.L

englishclasse.byrne63@gmail.com

Ilustraciones: **M. J. Ferris**. mariajosef181@gmail.com

Traducción al español: **Sergio R. Torres Matesanz**

Portada: **Paloma Planelles Baeza**

Rafael Torres Montero (editor)
ratomon.com
Alicante

Otros libros de Noreen J. Byrne

- *Cuentos y poemas infantiles en inglés: 17 poems for children - The pretty rat*
- *Tres novelas para practicar y aprender inglés: Tears of the rose - Henry Dwyer and the third wish—A miracle in El Campello*
- *Condicionales y adjetivos de cantidad ingleses*
- *Cómo superar una entrevista de trabajo en inglés (Get that job now) - Teaching English*

Los audios de este libro están disponibles **gratis** en readwithnoreen.com

Índice

There was almost, another sleeping beauty

By

Noreen J. Byrne

ONCE upon a time there lived a wonderful couple called Eva and Javier. They lived in a nice town called Yocla. They worked night and day to make the town pretty. They planted trees and flowers. Placed pretty containers around the town for people to put their rubbish into and handed refuse bags to people who were walking their dogs; so they could pick up the dogs excrement and not leave it on the ground.

Javier and Eva even made time to help less fortunate people who were disabled and they enjoyed cooking meals for their friends.

Because of all this, not only their neighbours, but all the people in Yocla elected them to be the King and Queen of their land.

This happy couple decided that they would like to have a family of at least two children, and within a year after this brave decision they produced a handsome baby boy.

Everyone cheered and danced when the first child was born. They named him Javito because he looked like a tiny copy of his father.

Javito thrived, became more and more intelligent and handsome as time went by and everyone adored him. They enjoyed watching him play in the park on his cycle or skateboard and every Sunday he'd play football with all the other boys in the town.

One day, after bringing in the logs from the garden and placing them on the big open fire: he told his mum Eva that he had seen fairies, boy fairies, and he asked her why there were no girl fairies in the beautiful town of Yocla. She told him the truth of course. "Javito, you are quite right my son, there are no girl fairies here because there are no little girls for them to play with."

* * *

So, you see dear reader, the town of Yocla had a big problem. There were no baby girls. In fact, there were no little girls anywhere in the land. People were really, really worried.

* * *

However, the queen had been keeping a secret. There was a tiny little baby girl happily growing in her tummy.

When this very special baby was fully formed in her mother's stomach she decided it was time to come out and join her family.

And so, the happy queen, after a few groans and

grunts, gave birth to a very precious, beautiful baby girl.

Javito was extremily happy and asked his parents to name his little baby sister: Natalia.

King Javier was overjoyed and gave the biggest party ever. He stopped working for a few days- now this was never heard of before because Javier was actually a workaholic and wanted only the very best for his family and the town-

He invited all the people, all the magicians and all the fairies that he knew would take great pleasure in giving the little princess a dowry of the very best things in life, like: kindness, intelligence, good health, wealth, happiness and beauty.

The king made his list of guests and decided not to invite a certain fairy named Olgea because this fairy had behaved very badly on a number of occasions in the past. He didn't want anything to spoil his new born baby daughter's party. "She must not be invited" he told his kind hearted queen, when she'd asked him to show pity for the bad fairy.

Previously, many moons ago, Olgea had placed a hex –a bad spell– on some of the royal family's friends who lived nearby in the town. She did bad things like this from time to time because she was jealous of people who had a little more than her or, who were popular and loved by their family and friends. Then, after she put the hex on them, these unfortunate people had had bad luck for many years.

Some, like twin boys, Rhys and Dylan, had woken up in the mornings with black noses, green toes and purple fingers and the colours would not wash off no matter how much they showered or scrubbed with soap. When they sat down to eat breakfast there was nothing to eat, because Olgea had sent fairy mice to their homes and these greedy mice had eaten the breakfast cereals, fruit, croissants, bread, milk and cakes, while the families were sleeping. Rhys and Dylan make mouse traps and caught two mice. However the mice had begged and begged to be released and so the good hearted twins felt sorry for the little creatures and set them free.

However, Olgea had magic powers of course. So, when she discovered she'd not been invited to the party she thought of a cruel plan. She looked into her long mirror and screeched. "I'll turn myself into a wicked witch. Witchy Wee, Witchy Woo, change me into Witchy Binny Poo".

The witch, dressed in a long black dress, black boots and with a bald head, which, was now covered in black shoe polish, cackled and hopped around the dirty sitting room like a crazy rabbit. She waved her black wicked wand and screamed: "Hey presto". She looked in the mirror and saw a funny faced Witchy Binny Poo staring back at her. She was smaller now and yellow, with fat little ears, black shiny nose and buttons for eyes. Her stomach was like a balloon and she couldn´t see her feet. "Jaa jaa", she screeched. "Everyone will love me, me meee, They will surly want me, they will give me all the attention and presents because I am gorgeous, cuddly and famous in Yocla, just like Witchy Binny Poo bear".

* * *

ON the day of the party all the people wore their best colourful clothes. The men wore snow-white shirts, black, beige, blue and even purple suits with wide belts around their waists and tall black hats.

Some looked very distinguished with gold or silver canes and all brought a gift for Natalia, and of course Javito, who, had been helping his mother to bath and care for his little sister.

Best of all were the fairies. They were super beautiful with dresses of silk and satin in pastel colours. They wore sandals of silver and gold on their feet and their hair was washed and shining in natural colours, brown, black, blond, grey, white and red.

Javito sat in the first coach with his proud parents. Princess Natalia was wrapped in a warm cream coloured blanket to keep her warm because she was only two months old and being the month of May the weather was not yet hot enough to go out without a coat or jacket. The big gold coach was the most expensive of all the coaches in the parade and four big black horses with shiny white socks, pulled and trotted along happily as the crowd cheered and musicians played in bands along avenues lined with sweet smelling flowers.

The trees, abundant with green leaves, seemed to smile as they gave fresh oxygen to the people of Yocla.

“Princess Natalia, Princess Natalia”, chanted all the people as they took photos of the royal couple and their two gorgeous children. “At last we have a little girl, a little girl, a pretty girl” sang an old lady as she played a harp while standing up in the following coach.

When they reached the palace the guards took the horses away to give them hay, carrots and fresh water, and the royal family and all the people went into a massive dinning room where they sat around beautiful white tables while waiters and waitresses served them plates of delicious salads with various sauces, buttered corn and large red succulent prawns to dip into pink tartar sauce; salmon, turkey, pure beef steaks served with various rices, creamed potatoes, peas, green beans, cauliflower and sautéed golden onions.

Javito was very happy because his grandmother Maria cooked his favourite pizza.

The servants served super fast and they were happy and so friendly to everyone. The fairies whispered to each other about the gifts they were going to bestow on the little princess and they only ate vegetables, lots of vegetables, as this is the habit of really good fairies.

Next to the queen sat a maid. It was her job to take care of the new baby. She smiled at the queen and the queen gave her the sleeping child to hold. The queen took up the silver knife and fork and began to eat. The maid held Natalia very gently in her arms and looked about the room at all the people trying to get a better view of the baby.

A fairy in rose-pink came closer to the child and very softly tapped three times on her little nose. "I grant you the fine gift of forgiveness" she said sweetly. And the maid smiled sweetly, the queen nodded, the King coughed, because he was eating too fast, Prince Javito chased a little green pea around his plate with a large fork saying "got you, got you" and princess Natalia slept.

People interrupted their eating to give gifts of toys, clothes, and jewellery to the royal family for giving them a princess and above all, a baby girl. Javier stopped torturing the pea and laughed aloud when he was handed a real gold Spinner with flashing lights and musical sounds. A tall elegant fairy came and gave Natalia the gift of good health and long life. A small fairy: this one was really tiny and could hardly reach up to tap the baby on the nose to grant the wish. "I give you the gift of pureness of heart, to make you the most caring and loving human in the land" And so on the fairies came and gave gifts so precious that they could not be bought, sold or even wrapped in gift paper.

The maid felt hungry and she picked up a fork with one hand and reached out to pierce a nice tender piece of turkey. As she brought it to her mouth she saw a very cute yellow bear coming towards her and the baby.

The king and queen were laughing and chatting with their guests and did not notice that a bear had not been invited to the party. Not even a Witchy Binny Poo.

Witchy Binny Poo smiled down at the sleeping child and said: "You have taken all my friends attention away from me. You will be far too popular, far too pretty and you will live far too long. But you will not enjoy a moment of it because with this poison needle I will put you into a super long sleep and you will sleep and sleep and sleep, just like the story of the sleeping beauty". The maid jumped up from her chair, clutching the baby to her breast, she screamed very very loud. Natalia woke up and screamed louder than the maid. The queen hiccoughed and then fainted, falling to the floor with a piece of prawn protruding from her lips. The king coughed even louder, for this time he'd eaten a bigger chunk of turkey and Javito –now this is the best part of the story– because Javito, saved his sister from a terrible fate. He jumped up so fast, caught the bear by the ear, and poured his glass of lemonade all over the jealous, and cruel Witchy the Pooh witch.

Now this was the worst thing you can do to a Binny Poo bear or a Witchy Binny Poo bear because the spongy yellow coat became all wet and soggy, the nose melted and the button eyes fell out and rolled across the floor and the tall colourful clown picked up the buttons and began to juggle with them.

The party went on and on until the next day and everyone went to bed, happy and contented.

Casi hubo otra bella durmiente

ERASE una vez que vivía una maravillosa pareja que se llamaba Eva y Javier. Vivían en un agradable pueblo llamado Yocla. Trabajaban día y noche para hacer el pueblo bonito. Plantaban árboles y flores. Ponían bonitos contenedores por todo el pueblo para que la gente pudiera depositar su basura en ellos y daban bolsas a aquellos que paseaban a sus perros para que pudieran recoger los excrementos de sus perros en vez de dejarlos en el suelo.

Javier y Eva incluso sacaban tiempo para ayudar a los más desfavorecidos que estaban inválidos, y disfrutaban cocinando para sus amigos.

Por todo esto, no solo sus vecinos, sino todo el pueblo de Yocla los eligieron para que fuesen rey y reina de ese país.

Esta feliz pareja decidió que les gustaría tener una familia de al menos dos hijos y menos de un año después de tomar esta valiente decisión tuvieron un precioso bebé.

Todo el mundo celebró y bailó cuando el primer hijo nació. Le llamaron Javito porque parecía una pequeña copia de su padre.

Javito creció, se volvió más y más inteligente y hermoso a medida que pasaba el tiempo y todo el mundo le quería. Disfrutaban viéndole jugar en el parque con su bicicleta o su monopatín y cada domingo jugaba al fútbol con los demás chicos del pueblo.

Un día, tras traer leña del jardín y ponerlos en la chimenea, le dijo a su madre Eva que había visto hadas, hadas chico, y le preguntó por qué no había hadas chicas en el bello pueblo de Yocla. Ella le contó la verdad, por supuesto. "Javito, tienes razón hijo mío, no hay hadas chica porque no hay niñas con las que puedan jugar".

* * *

Así que, ya ves, querido lector, el pueblo de Yocla tenía un gran problema. No había niñas. De hecho, no había niñas en todo el país. La gente estaba muy, muy preocupada.

* * *

Sin embargo, la reina guardaba un secreto. Tenía una pequeña niña creciendo felizmente en su vientre.

Cuando este bebé tan especial se formó en la barriga de su madre decidió que era hora de salir y unirse a su familia.

Y así, la feliz reina, tras unos cuantos gritos y quejidos, dio a luz a una preciosa, hermosa niña.

Javito estaba extremadamente feliz y preguntó a sus padres por el nombre de su hermanita: Natalia.

El rey Javier estaba exultante y dio la mayor fiesta jamás vista. Paró de trabajar por unos días, algo nunca oído antes, porque Javier era un adicto al trabajo y quería solo lo mejor para su familia y el pueblo.

Invitó a todo el mundo y todos los magos y todas las hadas que conocía estarían encantados de dar a la princesita como dote las mejores cosas de la vida, como amabilidad, inteligencia, buena salud, fortuna, felicidad y belleza.

El rey hizo su lista de invitados y decidió no invitar a cierta hada llamada Olgea porque esta hada se había comportado muy mal en diversas ocasiones en el pasado. No quería que anda arruinase la fiesta de su hija recién nacida. "No debe ser invitada" dijo a su bondadosa reina cuando ésta le pidió compadecerse del hada mala.

Anteriormente, hace muchas lunas, Olgea lanzó un maleficio, un hechizo maligno, a algunos amigos de la familia real que vivían cerca del pueblo. Hacía cosas malas como esta de vez en cuando porque tenía celos de las personas que tenían un poco más que ella o que eran populares y queridas por sus familias y amigos. Luego, tras maldecirles, estos desafortunados tenían mala suerte durante bastantes años.

Algunos, como los gemelos Rhys y Dylan, se levantaban por las mañanas con narices negras, dedos de los pies verdes y dedos de las manos púrpuras, y los colores no se iban por mucho que se lavasen o frotasen con jabón. Cuando se sentaban a tomar el desayuno no había nada que comer, porque Olgea había enviado ratones mágicos a sus casas y esos ratones egoístas se comían los cereales, fruta, cruasanes, pan, leche y bizcochos, mientras que las familias dormían. Rhys y Dylan hicieron trampas para ratones y atraparon a dos. Sin embargo, los ratones suplicaron y suplicaron para que los soltasen y los bondadosos gemelos se apiadaron de las pequeñas criaturas y las liberaron.

Sin embargo, Olgea tenía poderes mágicos, por supuesto. Así que, cuando descubrió que no había sido invitada a la fiesta, ideó un cruel plan. Miró en su gran espejo y chilló: "Me convertiré en una bruja malvada.

Witchy Wee, Witchy Woo, transfórmame en Witchy Binny Poo".

La bruja, vestida con un largo vestido negro, botas negras y con una calva cubierta con betún negro, soltó una carcajada y brincó por todo el salón como un conejo loco. Agitó su varita mágica negra y gritó: "Hey presto". Miró en el espejo y vio el alegre rostro de Witchy Binny Poo mirándola. Ahora era más pequeña y amarilla, con orejitas gruesas, una brillante nariz negra y botones en vez de ojos. Su estómago era como un globo y no podía ver sus pies. "Jaa jaa" chilló. "Todo el mundo me amará, a mí, a míiiii. Sin duda me querrán, me prestarán toda la atención y me darán regalos porque soy maravillosa, mimosa y famosa en Yocla, como el oso Witchy Binny Poo".

* * *

EL día de la fiesta, todo el mundo llevaba sus mejores y más vistosas ropas. Los hombres vestían camisas blancas como la nieve y trajes negros, beige, azules e incluso púrpuras, con cinturones gruesos alrededor de sus cinturas y sombreros de copa negros.

Algunos parecían muy distinguidos con bastones dorados o plateados y todos traían un regalo para Natalia y por supuesto para Javito, quien había estado ayudando a su madre a bañar y cuidar a su hermanita.

Las mejores de todos eran las hadas. Estaban bellísimas con vestidos de seda y satén de colores pastel. Llevaban sandalias de plata y oro en sus pies y su pelo estaba lavado y relucía con sus colores naturales, castaño, negro, rubio, gris, blanco y rojo.

Javito se sentó en la primera carroza junto a sus orgullosos padres. La princesa Natalia estaba envuelta en una manta de color crema para mantenerla calentita, ya que solo tenía dos meses y estaban en mayo, un mes en el que todavía no hace el suficiente calor como para salir sin un abrigo o una chaqueta. La gran carroza dorada era la más lujosa de todas las carrozas del desfile y cuatro grandes caballos negros con relucientes calcetines blancos tiraban del carro y trotaban alegremente mientras la multitud vitoreaba y los músicos tocaban a lo largo de las avenidas, cubiertas de flores de dulces fragancias.

Los árboles, repletos de hojas verdes, parecían sonreír mientras daban oxigeno fresco a la gente de Yocla.

"Princesa Natalia, princesa Natalia" coreaban todos mientras tomaban fotos de la pareja real y sus dos preciosos niños. "Al fin tenemos una niña, una pequeña niña, una preciosa niña" cantaba una viejecita mientras tocaba el arpa de pie desde la carroza de atrás.

Cuando llegaron al palacio, los guardias se llevaron a los caballos para darles heno, zanahorias y agua fresca, y la familia real y el resto fueron a un salón enorme donde se sentaron alrededor de bonitas mesas blancas mientras camareros y camareras les servían deliciosas ensaladas con varias salsas, maíz con mantequilla, suculentas gambas rojas con salsa tártara rosa para mojar, salmón, pavo, filetes de buey servidos con arroces variados, patatas cremosas, guisantes, judías verdes, coliflores, y cebollas doradas salteadas.

Javito estaba muy feliz porque su abuela María había cocinado su pizza favorita.

Los camareros servían súper rápido y eran muy amables con todos. Las hadas cuchicheaban las unas con las otras sobre los regalos ofrecer a la princesita y solo comían verduras, muchas verduras ya que es lo que hacen las buenas hadas.

Al lado de la reina estaba sentada una camarera. Su trabajo era cuidar de la recién nacida. Sonrió a la reina y la reina le dio al bebé dormido para que lo sostuviese. La reina tomó el cuchillo y el tenedor plateados y empezó a comer. La sirvienta sostenía a Natalia muy gentilmente en sus brazos y echó un vistazo a la habitación, a toda la gente intentando tener una buena vista del bebé.

Un hada vestida de rosa se acercó a la niña y, muy

suavemente, tocó tres veces su pequeña nariz. "Te concedo el buen regalo del perdón" dijo dulcemente. Y la doncella sonrió dulcemente, la reina asintió, el rey tosió, porque estaba comiendo muy rápido, el príncipe Javito cazaba un guisantito con su largo tenedor diciendo "te tengo, te tengo" y la princesa Natalia dormía.

La gente interrumpía su comida para dar regalos tales como juguetes, ropa o joyas para la familia real por darles una princesa y, sobre todo, una niña. Javier dejó de torturar al guisante y se rio a carcajadas cuando le dieron una rueca de oro puro con luces parpadeantes y sonidos musicales.

Una alta y elegante hada vino y otorgó a Natalia el regalo de una vida larga y llena de salud. Un hada pequeña, tan pequeña que apenas podía llegar a tocar la nariz del bebé para conceder el deseo. "Te concedo el regalo de la pureza de corazón, para hacerte la humana más bondadosa y cariñosa del país". Y así, las hadas venían y daban regalos tan preciosos que no podían ser comprados, vendidos o envueltos en papel de regalo.

La doncella se sintió hambrienta y cogió un tenedor con una mano y alcanzó a perforar una tierna pieza de pavo. Mientras se lo llevaba a la boca, vio un osito amarillo muy mono acercándose a ella y al bebé.

El rey y la reina estaban riendo y charlando con sus invitados y no se dieron cuenta que un oso no había sido invitado a la fiesta. Ni siquiera Witchy Binny Poo.

Witchy Binny Poo sonrió al bebé durmiente y dijo: "Me has quitado toda la atención de mis amigos. Serás muy popular, muy hermosa y vivirás demasiado tiempo. Pero no disfrutarás ni un momento de ello porque con esta aguja envenenada te voy a sumir en un sueño muy profundo y dormirás y dormirás y dormirás, como en la historia de la bella durmiente". La doncella saltó de su silla, apretando a la niña contra su pecho, y gritó muy muy alto. Natalia se despertó y gritó más alto que la sirvienta. La reina saltó un hipo y se desmayó, cayendo al suelo con una gamba sobresaliendo de sus labios. El rey tosió incluso más fuerte, ya que esta vez se había comido un pedazo más grande de pavo y Javito, ahora viene lo mejor de la historia, porque Javito salvó a su hermana de su terrible destino. Saltó rapidísimo, cogió al oso por la oreja, y vertió su vaso de limonada por encima de la envidiosa y cruel bruja Witchy Poo.

Esto era lo peor que se le podía hacer a los osos Binny Pooho Witchy Binny Poo, porque su esponjoso pelo amarillo se puso totalmente mojado y empapado, la nariz se le fundió y sus botones se cayeron de sus ojos y rodaron por el suelo y el alto y colorido payaso los recogió y comenzó a hacer malabares con ellos.

La fiesta siguió y siguió hasta el día siguiente y todos se fueron a la cama, felices y satisfechos.

A day's adventure

By

Noreen J. Byrne

YIPPY! A ray of sun. Nahia was extremely excited because the sun was shining and warming her pretty face. She was in Ireland and it was a very rainy country.

Because of all the rain the land was rich and green and she loved the smell of fresh grass and sweet scented flowers and of walking in the puddles and splashing soft water all around her.

The quiet, mild mannered nine year girl loved to sing and dance.

However, today she seemed distracted and in deep thought. She was so absorbed in the fine weather that she walked out the door in only her sandals and light sleeveless dress.

The birds were whistling and flying high above the trees and she became dizzy as she twirled around and around while watching them enjoying their merriment. Her long brown hair flew loosely around her face as she laughed aloud.

Suddenly Nahia heard barking. "Good morning Stitch,

come on boy, come to me" Nahia put out her arms and shouted to Mrs. Byrne's Bichon Frize dog.

"Are you coming with me today or not?" Woff woff barked Stitch.

The dog, the same age as herself, was very happy to see someone he loved and he could not resist the temptation to wag his tail and chase after her.

Now this dog Stitch is a very faithful little dog and he is a good companion for adventures and trekking because he has a strong sense of smell and a good sense of direction, which, is very lucky, because Nahia has no sense of direction whatsoever. Hence, her mother Corrina always worried about her, afraid that one day she would wander off and get lost.

The little girl was doing that now, wandering off towards the main pathway in the forest. A pathway where people went to stroll or to jog and keep fit.

When she was a few years younger she used to go there with her nana. She still loved walking along this path and often stood still, simply watching, while people jogged past carrying big bags on their backs. They wore thick boots and heavy jackets and she wondered how they could possibly carry it all and run at the same time.

This particular evening was in late September and a light wind was beginning to whistle through the trees, making a scary sound, and Nahia noticed that the darkness was falling earlier than usual. She shivered in her thin dress, It was made of fine lace and cotton and she had had it since her seventh birthday. She loved this dress, not only because it was pretty with pearl buttons, she cherished it because it had been given to her by her grand-ma Sue, her daddy´s mother. Everyone told her that she looked like her grandma Sue and this pleased her because Grandma Sue was a quiet English lady, who taught her many things and who loved her very much.

As Nahia walked, then skipped then bunny hopped along the path she let her mind go back to the last time she had seen her grand-ma Sue.

A smile brightened up her pretty face as she saw a colourful butterfly and then she heard a sound, like a baby crying. She stopped suddenly and waited. She didn't hear anything. Nothing. She thought that she must have imagined it. She bent and picked a big yellow daisy and as she did she Heard: "Meow, Meow" A cat! She couldn't see the cat but the sound was most defiantly that of a cat calling for help. "Where are you?" Shouted Nahia.

She walked faster looking all around her, from left to right and peering into the bushes. "Scaaaat". This time the sound was horrible. Like the cat was angry and spitting at something or somebody. Stitch growled and barked and chased after something running through the tall grass next to the path. Nahia saw the long brown tail of a cat protruding from the bushes. Stitch stopped running and stood barking at the cat. Nahia called out “come here Stitch. Leave that poor cat alone, you are frightening it”

But in reality, it was Stitch that was afraid because he had seen this particular fat cat before. It was a wild cat and it controlled all the other cats in the neighbourhood. In fact she was called Rola and her husband was called

Rolo.

Right now Rola was hissing like a cobra snake, her eyes were blazing with anger and suddenly she rolled on to her side and lay on the grass panting and mewing.

"Oh Holy Moly" lamented Nahia. "this poor creature is ill, or something."

Nahia crept closer to the cat and Stitch-not feeling very brave at the moment- walked quietly behind her. "Meow, Meeeoow, moaned the cat and suddenly she stood up, arched her back and...

* * *

Reader, can you guess what happened next?

* * *

A wet slippery ball of white fur fell from the cat's tummy onto the grass. It made a whimpering meowing sound. Rola the mother cat began to lick and clean the little kitten until it could stand up on its four little legs and say "meow" very weakly of course, because it was only a few minutes old, Again "Meaow" as if saying "Thank you."

Nahia was amazed at the sight of a cat giving birth to a little kitten and she knelt down beside Rola and gently stroked her head, at the same time saying "Good girl, good mother cat"

Then Rola the cat howled again, like a baby and out came two more little kittens. These two kittens were bigger than the first and were the colour of snow, white all over except for one of them had some black spots on its front paws. "Goodness Gracious me" shouted Nahia. "No wonder you were crying! You had three white kittens inside your tummy. How did they get in there? Who put them into your tummy? Did you swallow them or something?"

Stitch looked up at Nahia, thinking. "Hmm, surly she is not asking the cat how she came to have kittens in her tummy, is she? Doesn't she know that her husband, Rolo, has magic powers and while she was sleeping he sprinkled kitten dust on her tummy and the kittens grew inside her?"

Stitch barked and looked up at the sky. It was beginning to rain and Nahia did not have her coat, hat or Wellington boots.

The three kittens drank hungrily from their mothers breast milk and meowed.

Back at the house, Corrina was beginning to get worried. Nahia had been gone for over an hour and it was raining and getting darker by the minute. Corrina put on her coat, picked up the big old umbrella and went looking for her daughter.

Thunder roared and lightening flashed and Nahia picked up the two white kittens and began to run towards her home, all the time calling to Stitch and Rola to follow her. Rola was not a stupid cat. She opened her mouth and picked up her first born kitten by the fur on the back of its neck and then she followed Stitch and Nahia. They were very wet and cold. The darkness and the sound of thunder frightened them but they were brave because young lives had to be saved and getting the little kittens to a warm place was a priority.

In another part of the town Rolo was prowling around the back of the fish shop where he usually found some juicy pieces of fish to take home to his darling Rola. He knew she was going to give birth to some kittens so he wanted to keep her healthy and strong. In fact he was going to surprise her with a lovely new home. Yes, he was proud of this fact. Proud that he was going to be a daddy.

A week ago he proved how good a father he would be by chasing a family of squirrels from their home in the base of a big oak tree. The family of ten squirrels had to move all the way to a lower class area of the town and they surly didn't like that, but such is life on the streets of Dublin these days.

Now, Rolo had a delicious piece of salmon in his teeth and although he really wanted to eat it himself- he resisted the temptation and walked proudly to the new tree house, thinking that Rola would be there waiting patiently for him.

How disappointed he was when he found an empty house. He waited and waited and howled for his Rola but the sound of thunder in the sky drowned out all other sounds.

Corrina saw her daughter and Mrs. Byrne's dog running towards her. "Oh my poor darling" she yelled "come quickly" she placed the big umbrella over Nahia and did not notice that Nahia had two little kittens in her arms. In fact she didn't noticed Stitch or Rola with her wet kitten in her mouth as they trotted after them.

By the time the group of wet animals and people got to Nahia's home they were all tired and hungry.

The smell of baking bread and apple pie in the oven make their mouths water with desire. Corrina wrapped a big warm towel around Nahia and that was when she noticed the two wet crying kittens in Nahia's arms. "What? What is this? And this?" She looked at the little kittens. There was a big smile on her face as she took, first, the pure white kitten, then the white kitten with the black spots on the front paws. She took them into the warm kitchen and poured some warm milk into a bowl and placed it on the floor for them to drink. However the mother cat, Rola, wanted to feed the kittens with her own special breast milk so she meowed and meowed.

Corrina looked at Rola, and then at the kittens and then at Nahia, suddenly realizing what had actually happened.

Poor Nahia had said nothing as she was shivering with cold and was afraid that her mother was angry with her for wandering away from home and for being so very late. The big brown cat with the three kittens curled up next to the warm oven and fell asleep with her kittens happily sucking milk from her teats. Corrina sent Nahia to the bathroom and told her to take a warm shower and put on her pyjamas and then to come down to dinner.

And where was Stitch?

Stitch was wagging his tail in his own house as his beloved owner, Mrs. Byrne gave him a big juicy bone while she was telling him all about her busy day in her classroom and the funny moments she had spent with her students.

The rain slowed and eventually stopped. Corrina and Nahia slept peacefully in their beds while down in he kitchen Rola purred happily as her kittens slept safely on her tummy. But Rolo was not a happy cat. His Rola was missing and in frustration he ate the juicy piece of salmon, he prowled the forest and streets all night and went back to the tree house exhausted and lonely.

The next morning the sun came out and dried up all the grass and the streets were clean and fresh. Stitch was not a dog to stay at home and sit about doing nothing. He had chores to do. Bones to dig up, rubber toys to bury in Mrs. Byrne's garden and, and... well, he would think of something else to occupy his time as the day went on.

He had no interest at all in what occurred last night because cats were supposed to be his enemy but he had no idea why he was supposed to run and chase them like other dogs did. “Each to their own kind” was his motto. As he ran off down the street he saw big Rolo limping towards him. Now, usually when he saw big Rolo coming he would run away and hide because Rolo was a tough cat, a bad cat an angry cat. He was ready to run when he stopped and took a good long look at Rolo. “Hey dude” he barked, “don't you want to chase me”? Or better still, I'll chase you, as I'm supposed to do, earn myself some street credibility.”

Rolo sniffed around Stitch and whimpered. He could smell the scent of his darling Rola. Suddenly a thought

came to Stitch. (*Remember reader, I've already told you that Stitch is an extremely intelligent dog)

Stitch barked loudly into the big cat´s face. Rolo hissed and tried to scratch at Stitch eyes but Stitch was to fast. Then Stitch went behind Rolo and bit his tail causing the furious cat to howl and grown. Stitch began to run, he ran as fast as his little brave heart allowed him and he ran right into Corrina's garden and through the cat flap at the end of the hall door.

Rolo followed meowing and scratching at Stitch each time he got close enough to harm him. Corrina gasped as she saw the gorgeous little Bichon Frize bounding through the cat-flap and Nahia screamed when she saw big Rolo following. They stood staring as Rola ran towards Rolo, her kittens meowed because they´d been woken from their sleep. Nahia patted Stitch on the head for doing such a good deed. She went to the fridge and gave Rolo and Stitch a slice of thick succulent ham. “Well what on earth am I supposed to do with all of you” shouted Corrina. Nahia smiled and put her arms around her caring and loving mother. “Mum, you will do the right thing, you always do, Don't you?

La aventura de un día

YUJU! Un rayo de sol. Nahi a estaba emocionadísima porque el sol brillaba y calentaba su bello rostro. Estaba en Irlanda que es un país muy lluvioso. A causa de las lluvias, la tierra era fértil y verde y le encantaba el olor de la hierba fresca y el dulce aroma de las flores y caminar en los charcos y salpicar agua blanda a su alrededor.

A la tranquila y modesta niña de nueve años le encantaba cantar y bailar.

Sin embargo, hoy parecía distraída y absorta en sus pensamientos. Estaba tan absorbida por el buen tiempo que salió de su casa tan solo con sus sandalias y un vestido ligero sin mangas

Los pájaros estaban cantando y volando por encima de los árboles y se sintió mareada al dar vueltas y vueltas mientras los veía regocijarse. Su largo cabello castaño volaba alborotadamente alrededor de su cara mientras se reía en voz alta.

De repente, Nahia oyó unos ladridos. “Buenos días, Stitch, vamos chico, ven conmigo”. Nahia extendió sus brazos y gritó al bichón frisé de la señora Byrne.

“¿Vienes hoy conmigo o no?” “Guau guau”, ladró Stitch.

El perro, de su misma edad, estaba muy feliz de ver a alguien que quería y no pudo resistir la tentación de agitar su cola y perseguir a la niña.

Este perro, Stitch, es muy leal y un buen compañero de aventuras y viajes, ya que tiene un gran sentido del olfato y una buena orientación, lo que es una suerte, ya que Nahia no tiene el más mínimo sentido de la orientación. De ahí que su madre, Corrina, siempre esté preocupada por ella, temiendo que un día salga a deambular y se pierda.

La pequeña niña estaba haciendo precisamente eso, deambular hacia el camino principal del bosque. Un camino en el que la gente solía ir para pasear o correr para mantenerse en forma.

Cuando tenía unos años menos, solía ir allí con su abuela. Le seguía encantando caminar por ese sendero y a menudo se quedaba ahí parada, tan solo observando, mientras la gente pasaba trotando portando grandes bolsas a sus espaldas. Llevaban gruesas botas y pesadas chaquetas y se preguntaba cómo podían llevarlo todo y correr al mismo tiempo.

Esa tarde era finales de septiembre y una ligera brisa comenzaba a silbar a través de los árboles, haciendo un ruido siniestro, y Nahia se dio cuenta de que la oscuridad estaba llegando antes de lo normal. Tembló en su fino vestido; estaba hecho de encaje fino y algodón y lo tenía desde su séptimo cumpleaños. Le encantaba este vestido, no solo porque era muy bonito con botones de perlas, lo valoraba porque se lo había regalado su abuelita Sue, la madre de su papá. Todo el mundo le decía que se parecía su abuela Sue y esto le agradaba porque la abuela Sue era una señora inglesa tranquila, que le enseñaba muchas cosas y la quería mucho.

Mientras Nahia caminaba, daba saltitos y brincos por el camino, dejó que su mente retrocediese hasta la última vez que había visto a su abuelita Sue.

Una sonrisa iluminó su carita cuando vio una mariposa muy vistosa, y entonces escuchó un sonido, como de un bebé llorando. Se paró de golpe y esperó. No oía nada. Nada. Pensó que se lo debía de haber imaginado. Se inclinó y cogió una margarita amarilla cuando escuchó: “Miau, miau”. ¡Un gato! No podía ver al gato pero el sonido pararía el de un gato pidiendo auxilio “¿Dónde estás?”, gritó Nahia.

Caminó más rápido mirando alrededor, de izquierda a derecha y mirando en los arbustos. “Scaaaat”. Esta vez el sonido era horrible. Como si es gato estuviese enfadado y escupiendo a algo o alguien. Stich gruñó y ladró y persiguió algo corriendo a través de la alta hierba que había junto al camino. Nahia vio la larga cola marrón de un gato asomando entre los arbustos. Stitch dejó de correr y permaneció ladrando al gato. Nahia le llamó: "Ven aquí, Stitch. Deja a ese pobre gato en paz, lo estás asustando".

Pero en realidad, era Stitch el que estaba asustado porque ya había visto antes a este gato gordo en particular. Era un gato salvaje y controlaba a todos los demás gatos del barrio. De hecho, se llamaba Rola y su marido se llamaba Rolo.

Ahora, Rola estaba bufando como una serpiente cobra, sus ojos ardían con rabia y de repente rodó hacia un lado y se tumbó en la hierba jadeando y maullando.

"Oh Dios mío", se lamentó Nahia, "esta pobre criatura está enferma, o algo." Nahia se acercó cautelosamente cerca de la gata, y Stitch (no sintiendose muy valiente en ese momento) caminó tranquilamente detrás de ella. "Miau, miaaaaauuuu" gimió la gata y de repente se levantó, arqueó su espalda y...

* * *

Lector, ¿puedes adivinar qué sucedió a continuación?

* * *

UNA mojada y resbaladiza bola de pelo blanca cayó del

vientre de la gata a la hierba. Emitió un lloriqueo maullando. Rola, la madre gata, empezó a lamer y limpiar al gatito hasta que se pudo poner de pie con sus cuatro patas y dijo "miau", muy débilmente por supuesto, porque sólo tenía unos minutos de vida. De nuevo "miau" como si dijese "gracias".

Nahia estaba alucinada por la visión de una gata dando a luz a un pequeño gatito y se arrodilló al lado de Rola y suavemente acarició su cabeza, mientras decía "buena chica, buena madre gata".

Entonces Rola la gata aulló de nuevo, como un bebé y salieron dos pequeños gatitos más. Estos dos gatitos eran más grandes que el primero y eran del color de la nieve, totalmente blancos excepto uno de ellos, que tenía algunos lunares negros en sus patas delanteras.

"¡Dios bendito!" gritó Nahia. "¡No me extraña que estuvieses llorando! Tenías tres gatitos blancos en tu estómago. ¿Cómo han llegado ahí? ¿Quién los puso en tu barriguita? ¿Te los habías tragado o algo?"

Stitch miró a Nahia, pensando. "Hmm, no estará preguntando a la gata cómo llegó a tener gatitos en su barriga, ¿verdad? ¿No sabe que su marido, Rolo, tiene poderes mágicos y mientras dormía espolvoreó polvo de gatitos en su estómago y los gatitos creciendo dentro de ella?"

Stitch ladró y miró hacia el cielo. Estaba empezando a llover y Nahia no tenía su abrigo, gorro, o botas de goma.

Los tres gatitos bebían hambrientamente de la lecha materna y maullaban.

En su casa, Corrina se empezaba a preocupar. Nahia se había ido hace más de una hora y estaba lloviendo y oscureciendo cada vez más. Corrina se puso su abrigo cogió su gran y viejo paraguas y salió a buscar a su hija.

Los truenos retumbaban y los rayos destellaban y Nahia cogió a los dos gatitos blancos y comenzó a correr hacia su casa, llamando constantemente a Stitch y Rola para que la siguiesen. Rola no era una gata estúpida. Abrió su boca y cogió a su primogénito por el pellejo de su nuca y siguió a Stitch y Nahia. Estaban muy mojados y helados. La oscuridad y el sonido de los truenos los asustó, pero eran valientes porque tenían que salvar jóvenes vidas y llevar a los gatitos a un lugar cálido era una prioridad.

En otra parte de la ciudad, Rolo estaba merodeando por la parte de atrás de una pescadería donde solía encontrar jugosas piezas de pescado para llevárselas a su querida Rola. Sabía que iba a dar a luz a unos gatitos así que quería mantenerla saludable y fuerte. De hecho, iba a sorprenderla con un precioso nuevo hogar. Sí, estaba muy orgulloso de esto. Orgulloso de que iba a ser papá.

Una semana antes, demostró lo buen padre que sería echando a una familia de ardillas de su casa en la base de un gran roble. La familia de diez ardillas tuvo que mudarse a una zona de clase baja de la ciudad, y seguramente no les gustó eso, pero así es la vida en las calles de Dublín hoy en día.

Rolo tenía un delicioso pedazo de salmón en sus dientes y aunque realmente quería comérselo él solo, resistió la tentación y caminó orgullosamente a tu nueva casa árbol, pensando que Rola estaría esperándole pacientemente.

Qué decepción se llevó cuando se encontró con una casa vacía. Esperó y esperó y aulló por su Rola, pero el sonido de los truenos en el cielo ahogaba todos los demás sonidos.

Corrina vio a su hija y al perro de la señora Byrne correr hacia ella. "Oh, mi pobre tesoro" gritó "ven rápido" y puso el gran paraguas encima de Nahia y no se dio cuenta de que Nahia tenía dos gatitos en sus brazos. De hecho, ni siquiera reparó en Stitch o Rola con su gatito mojado en su boca mientras trotaban tras ellas.

Cuando el grupo de animales mojados y personas llegó a la casa de Nahia, todos estaban cansados y hambrientos.

El olor a pan horneándose y a tarta de manzana en el horno provocó la boca se les hiciera agua con deseo. Corrina envolvió en una toalla caliente a Nahia y fue entonces cuando se percató de los dos gatitos mojados llorosos en los brazos de Nahia. "¿Qué? ¿Qué es esto? ¿Y esto?" miró a los gatitos. Había una gran sonrisa en su cara cuando cogió, primero, al gatito totalmente blanco, y luego al gatito blanco con puntos negros en sus patas delanteras. Los llevó a la cálida cocina y vertió un poco de leche tibia en un bol y lo puso en el suelo para que bebieran. Sin embargo, la madre gata, Rola, quería alimentar a los gatitos con su propia leche especial materna, así que maulló y maulló.

Corrina miró a Rola y luego a los gatitos y luego a Nahia, y de repente se dio cuenta de lo que ocurría.

La pobre Nahia no había dicho nada ya que estaba tiritando de frío y tenía miedo de que su madre estuviese enfadada por haber paseado lejos de casa y volver muy tarde. La gran gata marrón se acurrucó con su tres gatitos al lado del horno caliente y se quedó dormida, con sus gatitos bebiendo leche de sus pezones felizmente. Corrina envió a Nahia al baño y le dijo de tomar una ducha caliente y ponerse su pijama y bajar después a cenar.

¿Y dónde estaba Stitch?

Stitch estaba meneando su cola en su casa ya que su amada dueña, la señora Byrne, le dio un gran y jugoso hueso mientras le contaba todo acerca de su ajetreado día en su clase y los momentos divertidos que había compartido con sus alumnos.

La lluvia amainó y eventualmente cesó. Corrino y Nahia dormían plácidamente en sus camas mientras que en la cocina Rola ronroneaba felizmente mientras que sus gatitos dormían a salvo acurrucados en su barriga. Pero Rolo no era un gato feliz. Su Rola no estaba y frustrado se comió el jugoso pedazo de salmón, merodeó por el bosque y las calles toda la noche y volvió a la casa árbol exhausto y solo.

A la mañana siguiente, salió el sol y secó la hierba, y las calles estaban limpias y frescas. Stitch no era un perro de quedarse en casa y sentarse sin hacer nada. Tenía cosas que hacer. Huesos que desenterrar, juguetes de goma que enterrar en el jardín de la señora Byrne y, y... bueno, ya pensaría en algo más para ocupar su tiempo según avanzase el día.

No tenía ningún interés en absoluto en lo que ocurrió la noche anterior porque los gatos se supone que debían ser sus enemigos, pero no tenía ni idea por qué se supone que debía correr y perseguirlos como los demás perros hacían. "A cada uno lo suyo" era su lema. Mientras bajaba corriendo por la calle, vio al gran Rolo renqueante acercándosele. Normalmente, cuando veía al gran Rolo acercarse, correría y se escondería porque Rolo era un gato duro, un gato malo, un gato enfadado. Estaba listo para echar a correr cuando se detuvo y echó un buen vistazo a Rolo. "Ey, tío" ladró, "¿no quieres perseguirme? O mejor aún, yo perseguirte, como se supone que debo hacer para ganarme un poco de credibilidad en las calles".

Rolo olisqueó alrededor de Stitch y gimoteó. Podía oler el aroma de su querida Rola. De repente, una idea se le vino a Stitch. (Recuerda, lector, ya te he dicho que Stitch es un perro extremadamente inteligente)

Stitch ladró muy alto en la cara del gran gato. Rolo bufó e intentó arañar los ojos de Stitch, pero Stitch era demasiado rápido. Entonces Stitch se puso detrás de Rolo y mordió su cola, haciendo que el furioso gato aullase y gruñese. Stitch empezó a correr, lo más rápido que su pequeño valiente corazón le dejaba y corrió hasta el jardín de Corrina y a través de la gatera del portón.

Stitch ladró alto en la cara del gran gato. Rolo siguió maullando y arañando a Stitch cada vez que se acercaba lo suficiente como para herirle. Corrina se quedó sin aliento cuando vio al precioso pequeño bichón frisé saltando por la gatera y Nahia gritó cuando vio que el gran Rolo le seguía. Se quedaron mirando mientras Rola corrió hacia Rolo, sus gatitos maullaban porque habían sido despertados de su sueño. Nahia acarició la cabecita de Stitch por haber hecho tan buena acción. Fue a la nevera y dio a Rolo y Stitch una gruesa porción de suculento jamón. "¿Y qué se supone que voy a tener que hacer con todos vosotros?" gritó Corrina. Nahia sonrió y abrazó a su atenta y cariñosa madre: "Mamá, harás lo correcto, siempre lo haces, ¿verdad?"

No Moon in Muchamiel

By

Noreen J. Byrne

THERE is a place in Muchamiel –"A lot of honey" is its name–. It's a special place that humans can not see and where animals cast their spells.

They hop and chase and scuttle, over rivers, lakes and grass. Tumbling, trotting, secretly plotting- who'll be next to catch bad Ass?

Behind green trees, below bramble bush with not a sound from the lark, the crow or the little Saoirse thrush. They've paws and claws and beaks and tails, well most of them, but not the snails.

Now, come with me, if you will, and we'll visit some creatures in Muchamiel.

* * *

HEY! Who is scratching on my shell?" Ciaran, the gallant tortoise asked loudly and angrily while putting his handsome head out of his large golden shell and looking about. First he looked left and then right. He couldn't see who the nuisance was so he looked up in the air in case it was Dylan and Rhys the hungry seagulls. But all he saw were clouds and the pretty yellow face of

Luna Grace the moon smiling down at him and winking playfully. “Humph,” he grumbled. “How can she be so happy at this time of the morning? Close your eyes woman, and go to sleep.”

He looked about him again, afraid that Mary Sheeba, the elegant tigress, might saunter by and accidentaly step on him, as she almost did a week ago. He peered all around him but nothing stirred. “Oh well, I must be imaging things in my old age,” he mumbled as he pulled his tired head back into his warm shell and closed his eyes.

Something warm, wet and slithery slid forward on the top of his shell and two little antennas tickled the top of his nose. “Atishoooo” sneezed Ciarán the tortoise, now angry once again. “Slippery! It's you! What are you doing up there on my newly glossed back, get off, get off this minute”

Slippery the snail was shivering uncontrollably and his little voice quivered as he begged. “Please Ciarán help me, please don’t be so selfish, it´s cold out here, and my shell is cracked, I´m freezing. Please let me get in there with you. I promise to give your shell a really good shine in the morning. You know how you love my high-gloss slime.”

Ciarán, being a kind hearted tortoise felt sorry for his little neighbour and very slowly he moved back into his shell- Actually, he had plenty of room in his shell and felt very happy that he had taken the advise of Irene the Care-Bear a week ago. Irene didn't need to loose weight and he'd told her so many times. “You’re pretty and kind and you're cuddly and we love you just the way you are” But being a real Care Bear, Irene insisted, so he´d gone with her to weight-ploppers and within four days of giving up eating fat worms and instead spending his time chasing after vitamin enriched grasshoppers, he´d actually lost a few ounces of fat from his belly and neck and felt more energetic too. Now he felt very comfortable in his fine shell. “Come on then, get in here under my armpit, and don´t snore or I´ll squash you into syrup, you little nuisance.”

While they slept peacefully something very strange was happening in that peaceful magical place. Someone was taking notes. This guardian of the animal kingdom was called Sara, a fairy squirrel with the cutest little face and nature ever known in this part of the world. Her lithe gosamer body flittered about here and there while her lovely long glossy tail floated gracefully behind her. In her tiny claw she held a quill pen and when she saw~or rather felt though her magic tail ~ that a good deed was being carried out, she'd swish and twirl and fly quickly to the scene of the action. Once there, she'd look, listen and hum quietly to herself as she took notes. She'd put the tip of the quilt-pen into her mouth and in doing this the magic ink would stick to the pen. Then she´d write on a very shiny piece of tree-leaf: first the names of the animal that did the good deed, and then the time, date and action. Then she´d fold it into a tiny piece and place in into the pocket of her glorious tail. She´d swish her magic wand, only once (for she didn’t believe in wasting precious time) and then: with a hop and a skip and a song on her lips, she'd fly back to her pine scented wooden home, sit on the ledge of a fallen palm tree and, ever so slowly , she's lick her curly tail until it shone like honey and run over to the little stream behind the fallen tree and study her pretty face in the mirror, twitching and stroking her tiny whiskers until it was just right, the way Tony hedgehog loved it. When she was happy with her appearance, she would scurry into his waiting arms, careful not to touch his spiny coat. For the next hour or so they would chat about their day's work.

Now, there are hedgehogs that have hard spiky quills so long and sharp that nothing, nor no one, can touch them. However, being a kind and caring hedgehog, Tony had his quills filed down every week so as his patients and his fiancée Sara didn't damage themselves on his armour.

Tony was a very busy hedgehog indeed because he was the vet, and his patients knew him by his first name because he was a very friendly hedgehog and had special ways of healing animals. He´d spent six long months in Uni-hedge studying to be the best animal doctor in Muchamiel, and it was worth it, because now all the animals in the land came to him with their problems and with their paws, claws, pouches and beaks full of succulent rich berries, carrots, apples and even pieces of cheese, bread, pasta and other nice things from Annie the cow and Darren the fox´s restaurant.

Foxy Darren was a real cute fox. When he was a cub his mum and dad were so afraid he would be caught and held for ransom that they used to cover his lovely golden curls and tail with cow manure to prevent anything bad happening to him. Foxy was clever, handsome and full of mischief. His kind aunt Barbara (Mrs. Fox) had built up a really nice restaurant and filled it with her super forest flavoured nuts, dates, berries, blackcurrants and seeds of every kind. All the animals came to her for advice or recipes. She loved cooking and having her family and friends sit around her log fires, singing songs of the forest.

So when Barbara retired to spend more time cruising up and down the rivers in her little curved log-boat, her nephew Foxy Darren and his wife (Annie the cow) took over the forest restaurant and with their little beautiful little bird Saoirse, they enjoyed days and nights feeding and drinking with all the animals and also the fairies and goblins that flittered about weaving their magical good and sometimes bad spells.

One winter evening, something very bad and scary happened in this place of beauty. Meerkat Sioban looked out of her office window and gasped! Her lovely bushy fur seemed to have turned florescent and her large blue eyes almost popped out of her tiny head in fright.

She used her long tail to balance as she stood upright to get a better view but fell over and cried out in pain as she broke the newly painted nail on her claw. She grabbed her chipfone and screamed for Gus Meerkat to come and see the horrible things that were happening outside her office.

Now Gus was a typical Meerkat and as everyone knows Meerkats are workaholics and great guardians of their families. Within mere minutes a screech of Spinner wheels (expertly made by Ciarán the super giant tortise) skidded to an abrupt stop.

Well, although gallant Gus tried with all his might to get into the office to save his beautiful wife; he couldn't, because, when he put his feet on the ground they became stuck and when he tried to free himself his tail became stuck to the ground too. He pulled and pulled and tried twisting about in a circle but it was no good. Out of breath and with tears running down his red face he whistled to his screaming wife to calm down. The meerkat whistle is a special whistle only known to meerkats and Siobhan stopped screaming at once.

All around were animals of every kind and all of them were terrified because they were stuck solid to the ground, unable to move. Even worse, Luna Grace the Moon was not up in the sky, beaming down at her friends as always at this time of night. No, she was lying on the cold ground and all around her: birds, mice, rats, frogs, toads, sloths, rabbits; hares, gerbils, tortoises and many many more animals of the fields and forests were standing still or lying down, crying, not knowing what was happening to them.

“Don’t come out” they called to Siobhan. “ If you come out she will put her hex on you too.”

Siobhan shivered and twitched her nose. She looked up at the black starless sky. “Where have all the stars gone?, and who did this terrible thing?” Suddenly there was a loud croak, then another. Holly the magnificiant crow looked down at the suffering animals on the ground and saw the tears on the meerkats faces. She flew to Siobhan and perched on the window-ledge. “Come on, you should be with Gus” She spread her big glorious wings around the shivering meerkat and swooping her up she flew down to where Gus was waiting with his claws held out to catch his wife. Holly placed Siobhan into his arms and away she flew in search of her best friend Sara.

But, sadly, there was a sudden storm and Holly toppled to the ground where she became stuck like all the animals around her. Tony Hedgehog tried vainly to reach her to repair her damaged wing but it was no good. The more he moved the more tired he became until he too was lying flat on the ground.

Silence filled the forest and land while all the animals cried themselves to sleep. All except three. Sara the magical fairy squirrel was searching everywhere for Tony. Her book of good deeds had finally been completed. She´d put it into a beautiful engraved box that held lots of rich treasures and trinkets that she’d stored away to give as presents.

Although the night was dark it suddenly became much

darker as a horrible howling sound came from the sky. SHHOOSSHH. A great big ugly eagle with red eyes and pointed nose hovered over the frightened animals. "CAAAWWW you wretched do-gooders, you think all your goodness and niceness went unnoticed, did you?"

This vicious, jealous creature was named Ragen, the enemy of all the good fairies. Her powers were woeful and harmful and when she was angered she brought fear and misery to everyone that was good and kind.

When Sara heard the terrible sound of Ragen's voice she screamed with fright, she knew that Tony and all his friends were in big trouble. She must find Goblin Cath-Eagle. Cath-Eagle had powers that Sara hadn´t. They would need the strongest of spells and hexes to get rid of this curse and expel Ragen from the land.

Ragen became furious when she saw the little squirrel flying through the air.

Ragen´s nasty spell was to stick everyone to the ground until they fell into a sleep forever and ever. But his fairy squirrel had wings.

"Go away or I will turn all your friends into bad vicious animals and they will eat each other." She cackled like an old witch. An evil look of glee crossed the nasty Eagle´s face as she peered down at the poor suffering animals on the ground. Sara cried out "No, No please don´t, I´ll go, I promise".

But it was too late. Ragen flapped her great wings causing a rotten smell to cover the land and all the animals changed into vicious greedy animals.

Sara yelled in horror as Tony hedgehog turned into a wolf with big teeth and red eyes. He raised his head and howled up at the moon but then he realised the moon was at his feet and looked down at her, blinking his eyes and utterly confused. Big glistening tears dropped from Sara´s eyes, however something like hot anger was growing inside her, giving her strength. She heard Darren the fox snarl like a dog as he glared at Annie the cow and Annie the cow was changing into a bull with big curvaceous horns. Celia Cheeta was quickly transforming into a serpent with a tongue so long it wrapped around Martin Lizzard, Tommy Racoon and John Badger who were staring in fright as they watched the horrible changes happening all around them. The meerkat and rodent families were all red and slimy, like giant snails slithering along the ground and snapping and sniffing at all the animals as they tried to get free.

Sara flew up into the sky and away home to her box of trinkets. When she got there she took the book of good deeds and put them in her tail pocket and then she swiched and turned and flew high over the mountains as fast as her gossamer wings would take her. Up and up she went until she found the magical animal she was searching for. "Please help us dear friend" she whispered to herself many times as she flew through the air.

He was in a cave with water running down the walls and mushrooms growing everywhere. The cave smelt damp and it felt cold but the little pomeranian dog with the heart of gold sat quietly, meditating.

When Sara the squirrel called his name he turned quickly and ran towards her. Kiskers Pureheart, bowed in front of her and: never once taking his intelligent brown eyes away from hers, he stood upright on his back paws, took her claw in his golden paw and kissed it tenderly. There was no need for words between these two beautiful creatures because their hearts were true and pure and their telepathic thoughts spoke only of good, of all that was precious on the earth and of that which they now had to do to free their friends.

Sara squirrel put her wand gently on her soul mates shoulder and together they flew to the place where Ragen had done her terrible deed.

The great big ugly eagle turned its red eyes towards Sara Squirrel and Kiskers Pureheart as they flew towards her, fearless and strong in their mission. Ragen felt a tremor of fear run along her spine as they landed and perched next to her. Kiskers on her left hand side and Sara on her right.

Sara´s wand was tiny but held power so strong that Ragen trembled when she felt it touch her side. She seethed with anger.

The sound of gnashing teeth and ugly words from below was too much for Sara to bear. She raised her magic wand, pointed it at Ragen´s breast and shouted. "In all that´s good, pure and true" release these animals from their torture and set them free, I command you." The big eagle hawked up flem and spat at Sara, but Kiskers raised his paw, it glowed brightly with powerful magic and he swatted the slime to the ground where it spread and spread and everywhere it covered turned white like snow. The sleeping animals were instantly released from their bondage.

Ragen the eagle screeched and tried to fly. She raised her great gigantic wings to put another hex on the free animals but Kiskers Pureheart placed his golden paw on her long talon. Ragen screeched louder than ever before as a great wave of pure white powder wrapped itself around her and trapped her in its magic. She couldn't move or even scream now as she was completely and tightly wrapped up in strong white gauze. From out of the dark sky swooped Cath-Eagle. She circled above the three figures on the wall- Sara the Fairy Squirrel, Ragen the nasty Eagle and Kiskers Pureheart.

Kiskers and Sara looked directly at each other and a silver line of purple electricity shot from their eyes like burning beacons. Turning away from each other and looking down to where the angry animals were growling, Sara and Kiskers directed their magical rods of lightening towards each of their neighbors and friends. Together they chanted words of love, of peace, off goodness and of purity and kindness.

It was not easy and it took a lot of power to change angry hearts to pure loving hearts again, but they did it and what a lovely sight it was as all the animals hugged and kissed each other with tears of happiness in their eyes. Gus meerkat placed Siobhan meerkat safely onto the now clean white ground but she quickly jumped back into his arms again.

Cath-Eagle the sentry for that particular part of Muchamiel, swooped down and with her long elegant beak she picked up Ragen -who was now wrapped tightly in a cocoon of white gauze-and with great flapping of her shiny blue wings she carried her far, far away to the land of Sleepy Nod.

There, Ragen the terrible Eagle would sleep for ever and ever, never more to bring harm and destruction to the land of Muchamiel.

When the moon and the stars once again shone down from the sky they looked brighter than ever before and all was well, happy and peaceful in the land of Muchamiel.

Sin Luna en Muchamiel

HAY un lugar en Muchamiel, un lugar especial que los humanos no pueden ver y donde los animales conjuran sus hechizos.

Saltan y brincan y juegan, por ríos, lagos y hierba. Cayendose, trotando, planeando en secreto quén será el próximo que busque en el juego del escondite,

Tras árboles verdes, bajo zarzas, no se oye el sonido de alondras, cuervos o de la pequeña Saoirse la torda. Tienen patas y garras y picos y colas, bueno, la mayoría de ellos, no así los caracoles. Ahora, ven conmigo, si quieres, y visitaremos a algunos criaturas en Muchamiel.

* * *

EY! ¿Quién está rascando mi caparazón?" preguntó a viva voz y enfadado Ciarán, la galante tortuga macho, mientras sacaba su bella cabeza fuera de su gran concha dorada, mirando a su alrededor. Primero miró a la izquierda y luego a la derecha. No podía ver quién le molestaba, así que miró hacia arriba por si fuesen Dylan y Rhys, las hambrientas gaviotas. Pero todo lo que vio fueron nubes y la hermosa cara amarilla de Luna Grace, la Luna, sonriéndole y guiñándole un ojo juguetonamente. "Humph" refunfuñó. "¿Cómo puede estar tan feliz a estas horas de la mañana? Cierra los ojos mujer, y vete a dormir".

Miró a su alrededor otra vez, temerosa de que Mary Sheeba, la elegante tigresa, pudiese pasear por ahí y pisarle accidentalmente como casi hizo hace una semana. Miró alrededor, pero nada se movía. "Oh bueno, debo estar imaginándome cosas a mi avanzada edad" murmuró retrayendo su cansada cabeza en su cálido caparazón y cerró los ojos.

Algo caliente, mojado y resbaladizo se deslizó por encima de su concha y dos pequeñas antenas cosquillearon su nariz. "Achúuuuuus" estornudó Ciarán la tortuga, ahora enfadado de nuevo. "¡Resbaladizo! ¡Eres tú! ¿Qué estás haciendo ahí encima de mi recién pulida espalda? Bájate, bájate ahora mismo".

Resbaladizo, el caracol, estaba temblando incontrolablemente y su pequeña voz se estremecía al suplicar: "Por favor Ciarán, ayúdame, por favor no seas egoísta, hace frío fuera, y mi caparazón está resquebrajado, me estoy helando. Por favor, déjame meterme ahí dentro contigo. Te prometo dar brillo a tu caparazón por la mañana. Sabes cómo te gusta mi baba de alto brillo".

Ciarán, que era una tortuga macho con un gran corazón, sintió pena por su pequeño vecino y muy lentamente volvió a su caparazón. En realidad, tenía mucho espacio en su caparazón y se sintió muy feliz de haber llevado a cabo el consejo que le dio Irene la osa amorosa hace una semana. Irene no necesitaba perder peso y se lo dijo una y otra vez. "Eres bonita y amable y tierna y te amamos tal y como eres". Pero siendo una verdadera osa amorosa, Irene insistió en acompañarle a hacer pesas, y en menos de cuatro días de haber renunciado a comer gusanos gordos y en su lugar invertir el tiempo en cazar saltamontes repletos de vitaminas, había perdido un par de kilos de grasa de su estómago y cuello y se sentía más energético. Ahora se sentía muy cómodo en su bonito caparazón. "Vamos, ponte aquí debajo de mi sobaco, y no ronques o te haré puré, pequeño incordio".

Mientras dormían plácidamente, algo muy extraño estaba sucediendo en ese mágico lugar lleno de paz. Alguien estaba tomando notas. La guardiana del reino animal se llamaba Sara, un hada ardilla con la carita más mona y la mayor naturalidad que jamás se conoció en esa parte del mundo. Su flexible cuerpo revoloteaba por aquí y por allá mientras su adorable, brillante y larga cola flotaba graciosamente detrás de ella. En su diminuta garra sostenía una pluma, y cuando vio (o, mejor dicho, sintió a través de su cola mágica) que una buena obra estaba ocurriendo, salió disparada haciendo piruetas y volando rápidamente hasta la escena de la acción.

Una vez allí, miró, escuchó y canturreó mientras tomaba notas. Puso la punta de la pluma en su boca y haciendo esto la tinta mágica se adhirió a ella. Entonces, escribió en una reluciente hoja de árbol: primero, el nombre del animal que hizo la buena obra, y luego la hora, fecha y acción. Después, la dobló muchas veces y la puso en el bolsillo de su gloriosa cola. Agitó su varita mágica una sola vez (ya que no le gustaba gastar un valioso tiempo). Entonces, con un salto, un brinco y una canción en sus labios, voló de vuelta a su hogar de madera con olor a pino. Se sentó en el borde de una palmera caída, y, lentamente, lamió su cola enroscada hasta que relució como la miel. Corrió hasta el pequeño arroyo detrás del árbol caído y admiró su preciosa carita en el espejo, sacudiendo y acariciando sus pequeños bigotes hasta que estuvieron perfectos, justo como a Tony el erizo le gustaba. Cuando estuvo satisfecha con su aspecto, se escabulló hasta sus acogedores brazos, con cuidado de no tocar su espinoso pelaje. Durante una hora estuvieron hablando sobre su día de trabajo.

Hay erizos que tienen púas tan duras y largas que nada ni nadie puede tocarlas. Sin embargo, siendo un atento y amable erizo, Tony se limaba cada semana sus púas para que sus pacientes y su prometida Sara no se hiriesen con su armadura.

Tony era un erizo muy ocupado ya que era veterinario, y sus pacientes le conocían por su nombre de pila porque era un erizo muy amigable y tenía una forma especial de curar a los animales. Pasó seis largos meses en la universidad para erizos estudiando para ser el mejor doctor animal de Muchamiel, y valió la pena. Ahora todos los animales del reino acudían a él con sus problemas y sus patas, garras, bolsas y picos llenos de suculentas bayas, zanahorias, manzanas e incluso pedazos de queso, pan, pasta y otras cosas del restaurante de Annie la vaca y Darren el zorro.

Darren el zorrito era un zorro muy mono. Cuando era un cachorro, su mamá y su papá tenían miedo de que lo raptaran y pidieran un rescate. Así que solían cubrir sus rizos dorados y su cola con estiércol de vaca para que no le ocurriese nada malo. El zorrito era inteligente, apuesto y muy travieso. Su bondadosa tía Bárbara (la señora Zorra) había montado un bonito restaurante y lo llenó con sus supersabrosas nueces del bosque, dátiles, bayas, grosellas y semillas de todo tipo. Todos los animales venían a verla para que les diese consejo o recetas. Le encantaba cocinar y que su familia y amigos se sentasen alrededor de una hoguera, cantando canciones del bosque.

Así que cuando Bárbara se retiró para pasar más tiempo de crucero por los ríos en su pequeño bote de madera, su sobrino Darren el zorrito y su mujer, Annie la vaca, tomaron las riendas del restaurante del bosque, con su hermoso pajarito Saoirse. Disfrutaban día y noche dando de comer y beber a los animales, y también a las hadas y los goblins que revoloteaban por ahí creando sus buenos (y malos) hechizos mágicos.

Una tarde de invierno, algo muy malo y aterrador sucedió en este bello lugar. Siobhan la suricata miró por la ventana de su oficina y se quedó sin aliento: su frondoso pelaje pareció haberse vuelto fluorescente y sus grandes ojos azules casi se salieron de sus órbitas de puro pavor.

Usó su larga cola para mantener el equilibrio mientras intentaba tener una mejor vista, pero se cayó y gritó de dolor al romperse una uña recién pintada. Cogió su teléfono patata y pidió a Gus el suricato que viniese para ver las cosas horribles que sucedían fuera de la oficina. Gus era un suricato típico y todo el mundo sabe que las suricatos son adictos al trabajo y grandes guardianes de su familia.

En apenas unos minutos, se oyó un chirrido de ruedas derrapando, hecho expertamente por Ciarán la gigantesca tortuga, al detenerse abruptamente. Pues bien, aunque el galante Gus trató por todos los medios de acceder a la oficina para salvar a su bella esposa, no pudo, porque, cuando puso los pies en el suelo, se quedaron pegados y cuando trató de liberarse, su cola se quedó pegada al suelo también. Tiró y tiró, e intentó girar, pero no sirvió para nada.

Sin aliento y con lágrimas corriendo por su cara colorada, silbó a su mujer que estaba gritando para que se calmase. El silbido de los suricatos es un silbido especial que solo conocen las suricatas y Siobhan dejó de gritar.

Alrededor había animales de todo tipo y todos ellos estaban aterrados porque estaban completamente pegados al suelo, incapaces de moverse. Aun peor, Luna Grace, la Luna, no estaba en el cielo, irradiando a sus amigos como siempre hacia a esta hora de la noche. No, estaba yaciendo en el frío suelo, y con ella, todo a su alrededor: pájaros, ratones, ratas, ranas, sapos, perezosos, conejos, liebres, jerbos, tortugas y muchos, muchos más animales del campo y del bosque estaban inmóviles o tumbados, llorando, sin saber qué les estaba sucediendo.

"No salgas" dijeron a Siobhan. "Si sales, te maldecirá a ti también".

Siobhan tembló y arrugó su nariz. Miró al negro cielo sin estrellas. "¿Adónde se han ido todas las estrellas? ¿Quién ha hecho algo tan terrible?"

De repente, se oyó un fuerte graznido, seguido de otro. Holly, la magnífica cuerva miró abajo a los animales sufriendo en el suelo, y vio las lágrimas en los rostros de los suricatos. Voló hasta Siobhan y se posó en la cornisa. "Vamos, deberías estar con Gus". Extendió sus enormes y gloriosas alas alrededor de la temblorosa suricata y bajó en picado hasta donde se encontraba Gus con sus garras listas para coger a su mujer. Holly puso a Siobhan en sus brazos y voló en busca de su mejor amiga Sara.

Pero, por desgracia, comenzó una repentina tormenta y Holly cayó al suelo donde se quedó pegada como el resto de animales alrededor de ella. Tony Erizo intentó en vano de alcanzarla para reparar su ala herida. Cuanto más se movía, más cansado se sentía, hasta que se encontró también tirado en el suelo.

Un silencio invadió el bosque y la tierra mientras todos los animales lloraban para dormir. Todos excepto tres. Sara, la ardilla hada, buscaba por todas partes a Tony. Su libro de buenas obras por fin había sido completado. Lo puso en una caja con un bonito grabado que contenía muchos tesoros y baratijas que había guardado para tener como regalos.

Aunque la noche era oscura, de repente se volvió mucho más oscura cuando un horrible aullido vino desde el cielo. "Shhoooooshh". Un águila enorme y fea con ojos rojos y picuda nariz planeó sobre los animales asustados. "Caaawww, miserables bienhechores, os creíais que toda vuestra bondad y buenas acciones pasarían desapercibidas, ¿verdad?"

Esta despiadada y envidiosa criatura se llamaba Ragen, la enemiga de las hadas buenas. Sus poderes eran deplorables y dañinos, y cuando se enfurecía, traía terror y miseria a todos los que habían sido buenos y amables.

Cuando Sara oyó el terrible sonido de la voz de Ragen, gritó aterrada: sabía que Tony y sus amigos estaban en graves problemas. Debía encontrar a la goblin Cath-Águila. Cath-Águila poseía poderes que Sara no tenía. Necesitarían el más poderoso de los hechizos y maleficios para librarse de esta maldición y expulsar a Ragen del reino.

Ragen se puso furiosa cuando vio a la pequeña ardilla volar por el cielo.

El asqueroso encantamiento de Ragen consistía en pegar a todos al suelo hasta que cayesen en un sueño eterno. Pero el hada ardilla tenía alas.

"Vete o convertiré a todos tus amigos en malos y atroces animales y se comerán los unos a los otros". Soltó una carcajada como lo haría una vieja bruja. Una malvada mirada llena de júbilo se formó en el rostro de la repugnante águila al mirar a los pobres animales sufriendo en tierra. Sara gritó: "No, por favor, no lo hagas, iré, lo prometo".

Pero era demasiado tarde. Ragen batió sus poderosas alas provocando que un olor a podrido cubriese el reino y los animales se transformaran en feroces y avariciosas bestias.

Sara chilló horrorizada al ver a Tony Erizo convertirse en un lobo con grandes fauces y ojos rojos. Levantó la cabeza y aulló a la Luna, pero entonces se dio cuenta de que la Luna estaba a sus pies y la miró, parpadeando en total confusión. Grandes lágrimas resplandecientes brotaban de los ojos de Sara. Sin embargo, algo como una furia ardiente se estaba formando dentro de ella, dándole fuerzas.

Escuchó a Darren el zorro gruñir como un perro al ver que Annie la vaca se estaba convirtiendo en un toro con grandes y curvados cuernos. Celia la guepardo se estaba transformando rápidamente en una serpiente con una lengua tan larga que envolvió a Martín el lagarto, Tommy el mapache y John el tejón, que estaban mirando con miedo los horribles cambios sucediendo a su alrededor. Los suricatos y los roedores estaban todos rojos y viscosos, como caracoles gigantes deslizándose por el suelo y olisqueando a todos los animales mientras intentaban liberarse.

Sara voló por el cielo hasta su casa para llegar hasta su caja de baratijas. Cuando llegó allí cogió su libro de buenas obras y lo puso en el bolsillo de su cola y entonces se giró y voló por encima de las montañas lo más rápido que sus alas de telaraña le dejaron. Subió y subió hasta que encontró al animal mágico que buscaba. "Por favor, ayúdanos, querido amigo", susurró unas cuantas veces mientras surcaba el cielo.

Estaba en una cueva con agua corriendo por las paredes y champiñones creciendo por todas partes. La cueva olía a humedad y era muy fría, pero el pequeño perro pomerania con un corazón de oro estaba sentado tranquilo, meditando.

Cuando Sara la ardilla pronunció su nombre, se dio rápidamente la vuelta y corrió hacia ella. Kiskers Corazonpuro se inclinó delante de ella y, sin quitar sus ojos marrones de los suyos, se puso de pie sobre sus patas traseras, tomó su garra en su pata dorada y la besó con ternura.

No había necesidad de intercambio palabras entre estas dos bellas criaturas porque sus corazones eran puros y sus pensamientos telepáticos hablaban sólo de cosas buenas, de todo lo precioso en la Tierra y de lo que debían hacer ahora para liberar a sus amigos.

Sara la ardilla puso se varita suavemente en el hombro de su alma gemela y juntos volaron al lugar en el que Ragen había cometido su terrible obra.

La horrible águila enorme giró sus ojos rojos hacia Sara la ardilla y Kiskers Corazonpuro, quienes volaban hacia ella, sin miedo y determinados en llevar a cabo su misión. Ragen sintió una sacudida de miedo recorrerle por dentro cuando aterrizaron y se situaron a su lado, Kiskers a la izquierda y Sara a la derecha.

La varita de Sara era pequeña, pero contenía un poder tan inmenso que Ragen tembló cuando la sintió tocarle. Una rabia incontrolada se apoderó de ella.

El rechinar de dientes y feas palabras susurradas era demasiado para que Sara lo pudiese soportar. Alzó su varita mágica, la apuntó al pecho de Ragen y gritó: "Por todo lo que es bueno, puro y auténtico, suelta a estos animales de su tortura y libéralos, te lo ordeno". La gran águila carraspeó y escupió a Sara, pero Kiskers levantó su pata, que resplandeció con poderosa magia y golpeó la sustancia pegajosa en el suelo, y su magia se extendió y se extendió y allá donde cubría se volvió blanco como la nieve. Los animales durmientes fueron liberados inmediatamente de sus ataduras.

Ragen la águila chilló e intentó volar. Alzó sus gigantescas alas para lanzar otro maleficio a los animales libres, pero Kiskers Corazonpuro puso su pata dorada en su larga garra. Ragen chilló más fuerte que nunca cuando una ola de polvos blancos puros la envolvió y la atrapó en su magia. Ya no podía moverse o gritar siquiera ya que estaba firmemente atrapada por un fuerte tejido blanco. Del cielo oscuro surgió Cath-águila. Dio vueltas por encima de las tres figuras en el muro: Sara la ardilla hada, Ragen la repugnante águila, y Kiskers Corazonpuro.

Kiskers y Sara se mirando el uno al otro y una luz de esperanza de electricidad púrpura brilló en sus ojos como faros. Dándose la vuelta y mirando abajo donde estaban los furiosos animales gruñendo, Sara y Kiskers dirigieron sus bastones de luz mágicos hacia sus vecinos y amigos. Juntos recitaron palabras de amor, de paz, de bondad y de pureza y gentileza.

No era fácil, y tomó mucho poder cambiar corazones furiosos en corazones puros llenos de amor de nuevo, pero lo hicieron y qué hermosa visión fue ver a todos los animales abrazarse y besarse entre ellos con lágrimas de felicidad en sus ojos. Gus el suricato puso a Siobhan la suricata a salvo en el ahora limpio y blanco suelo, pero rápidamente volvió a saltar a sus brazos.

Cath-águila, la centinela de esa parte de Muchamiel, bajó y con su largo y elegante pico cogió a Ragen (quien estaba envuelta firmemente en un capullo de tejido blanco) y con una gran batida de sus brillantes alas azules se la llevó muy, muy lejos hasta el Reino Durmiente.

Ahí, Ragen la terrible Águila dormiría por siempre, para no volver a traer dolor y destrucción a la tierra de Muchamiel.

Cuando la Luna y las estrellas brillaron de nuevo en el firmamento, lucían más brillantes que nunca y todo volvió a estar bien, feliz y en paz en la tierra de Muchamiel.

www.ingramcontent.com/pod-product-compliance
Ingram Content Group UK Ltd.
Pitfield, Milton Keynes, MK11 3LW, UK
UKHW041642190726
13854UKWH00006B/2651